D0096488

Casualty!

Peter Viney

BOOK SOLD
NO LONGER R.H.P.L.
PROPERTY

RICHMOND HILL
PUBLIC LIBRARY

NOV 25 2015

CENTRAL LIBRARY
905-884-9288

Garnet

EDUCATION

RICHMOND HILL
PUBLIC LIBRARY
NOV 25 2015
CENTRAL LIBRARY
905-884-9288

Peter Viney – author of this book, and Series Editor of the Garnet Oracle Readers – has over 40 years' experience teaching English and writing ELT materials. He now combines his writing with lecturing and teacher-training commitments internationally. He has authored and co-authored many successful textbook series and developed a wide range of highly popular video courses. Peter has been series editor and author on a number of graded reader series, and has also published with Garnet Education the highly popular *Fast Track to Reading*.

Published by
Garnet Publishing Ltd.
8 Southern Court
South Street
Reading RG1 4QS, UK

www.garneteducation.com

Copyright © Garnet Publishing Ltd 2014

The right of Peter Viney to be identified as the author of this work has been asserted in accordance with the Copyright, Design and Patents Act 1988.

All rights reserved.

No part of this publication may be reproduced, stored in a retrieval system, or transmitted in any form or by any means, electronic, mechanical, photocopying, recording or otherwise, without the prior permission of the Publisher. Any person who does any unauthorized act in relation to this publication may be liable to criminal prosecution and civil claims for damages.

ISBN 978 1 90757 529 7

Photocopying and duplication
The resources in the additional resources section may be photocopied for use by the purchasing institution and the students in its classes. They may not be copied for use by staff or students in other institutions. The CDs may not be duplicated under any circumstances.

British Cataloguing-in-Publication Data
A catalogue record for this book is available from the British Library.

Production
Series editor: Peter Viney
Editorial: Clare Chandler, Lucy Constable

Design and layout: Mike Hinks
Illustration: Doreen Lang

Every effort has been made to trace copyright holders and we apologize in advance for any unintentional omission. We will be happy to insert the appropriate acknowledgements in any subsequent editions.

Printed and bound in Lebanon by International Press: interpress@int-press.com

1 Emergency!

'Gail, you must have a rest. Go and have a coffee.'

Gail looked round. Dr Kennedy was standing behind her. She looked down at the man in the bed.

'He's OK,' said Dr Kennedy. 'I'm here now. Go on, you're tired.'

Gail smiled. 'Are you sure?' she said.

'You started work six hours ago. You can't work all night! Come back in twenty minutes.'

'But it's Saturday night. We're always very busy on Saturdays ...'

'Go on!' said the doctor.

Gail looked at him. He was tired too. Saturday was always busy in A & E – the accident and emergency department at Midhurst Central Hospital. There were road accidents, fights and all the other emergencies.

'All right,' she said. 'I'm going.'

She walked to the coffee machine and bought a cup of coffee. Then she went to the small office for nurses, and sat down. The coffee wasn't very good. She didn't like coffee from machines. Gail took a newspaper from the table, and opened it. It was *The Daily News.* She read one or two stories. They weren't very interesting. Then she stopped. There was a big picture of Alex Hayle on the page. She liked his new record ... what was it? Ah, yes, *Midnight Party.* She read the story.

Gail looked at the clock on the wall. The concert finished at midnight. It was half past twelve now. It was Sunday morning. Gail looked at the next page. Suddenly she heard the bell. There was an emergency!

New Face in Midhurst: Concert tonight

Alex Hayle is singing in Midhurst tonight! Alex was the singer in the boy band *New Face* until last year. *New Face* had six top ten hits in Britain, and they sold over twenty million CDs in the United States. Twenty-three-year-old Alex left the group last September for a solo career. All his new songs were big hits, and he is now the biggest star in the country. His concert is at the Midhurst United football stadium at nine o'clock. There are 30,000 seats in the stadium, and it will be full.

She hurried back into the accident and emergency department. Dr Kennedy was running towards the door.

'An ambulance is arriving … there was a bad car crash! They're bringing a serious casualty in,' he shouted. 'Come on!'

Gail ran after him. Two paramedics were coming through the door with a stretcher. She looked down at the man on the stretcher. She couldn't see his face. There was a lot of blood.

'Hurry! We think he broke his back,' shouted a paramedic, 'and he's cut his face badly. He needs more blood! Bring some blood, quickly!'

They carried the stretcher towards the lift. Dr Kennedy turned to Gail.

'It's his back. We'll need a specialist,' he said. 'Call Dr Casey.'

Gail ran to the phone. She called Dr Casey. The paramedics took the man on the stretcher up to the operating theatre.

'Gail,' said Dr Kennedy, 'I want you to get some information about him. His friends are over there.'

'Don't you need me in the operating theatre?' she asked.

'No,' said Dr Kennedy. 'Just get the information.'

2 The man with the cigar

Gail walked towards the door. Two men were standing there. One was short and heavy. He was smoking a cigar. The other was a very tall man. He was wearing a long black coat.

'Excuse me,' said Gail. 'You can't smoke in here. This is a hospital.'

The short man looked at her for a moment.

'What?' he said.

'You can't smoke in here. You must know that.'

'I'm right by the door.' He moved back a short way. 'Now I'm outside.'

'You can't smoke there, either.'

The man threw his cigar on the ground and put his foot on it. 'Is that all right, nurse?' he said.

Gail looked at the cigar. Her face was red. 'I need some information about your friend,' she said. 'It's for the hospital. It's important. Can I ask you some questions?'

'Questions?' said the man. 'What kind of questions?'

'First, what's his name?' said Gail.

The man laughed. 'You don't know?' he said. 'You're the only person in the country that doesn't know!'

'No, I don't know,' said Gail, 'and I'm very busy. So please answer. What is his name?'

The short man looked at the other man. 'She doesn't know Alex,' he said.

'Everybody knows Alex,' said the other man.

'Are you going to answer me or not?' said Gail.

The man looked straight at her. She didn't like his eyes. They were small and grey and very cold. 'That, my darling, is Alex Hayle. That's A-L-E-X H-A-Y ...'

'Thank you,' said Gail. 'I can spell it.' She was thinking about the story in the newspaper. Alex Hayle, the rock singer! 'How old is he?'

The man laughed. 'He's twenty-seven,' he said.

'In my newspaper it says he's twenty-three,' said Gail.

'Yeah, yeah,' said the man. 'In the newspaper he's twenty-three. In the hospital, he's twenty-seven. That's really his age. Is that OK, darling?'

'Don't call me darling.'

'Sorry ... darling.'

'Where does he live?'

'Alex? Here ... and there.'

'I must have his address,' said Gail.

'Put the Ritz Hotel, 150 Piccadilly, London. He was there yesterday. He was going there tonight.'

Gail wrote the address. 'Do you know the postcode?'

'No. Look on the Internet.'

'And who is his next of kin?'

'His what?' said the short man.

'His next of kin ... the closest person in his family. His wife, or his mother or father,' said Gail. 'We need the information because ...'

'He hasn't got a wife. His mother and father are dead. Write my name down ... I'm his manager.'

'Has he got any brothers or sisters? We need the name of someone in his family.'

'Look, darling, he hasn't got any family. Do you understand? Put my name.'

The short man's face was very near Gail. She could smell the cigar smoke.

'All right,' she said, 'tell me your name and address.'

'Clarence Tucker. Tucker International Managers Limited. 573 Shaftesbury Avenue, London. That's L-O-N-D-O ...'

'Very funny,' said Gail. 'Are you his manager?'

'I told you that,' said the man. 'Yes, I'm his manager. Are you finished?'

'One more question,' said Gail. 'What's his religion?'

He laughed. 'Religion? Alex?'

'Yes,' said Gail, 'religion. Which church does he go to? Or which ...'

The short man turned to the tall man. 'What religion is Alex?' he asked.

'I don't know.'

'Write "Don't know", darling. So you're finished now.'

'Yes,' said Gail. 'Thank you, Mr Tucker. Don't worry about Mr Hayle. Dr Casey is looking after him. She's a wonderful doctor.'

'Is she?' said the man. 'Well, I want the *best* doctor. Alex is in the middle of a fifty-million-dollar world concert tour. I don't want a doctor in a little hospital in a little town like Midhurst.'

'What happened to him?' asked Gail.

The tall man spoke. 'Alex drove from the concert. He was very tired. Clarence told him to come with me, but he didn't. He was driving too fast, and he crashed the car and ...'

'Be quiet, Roger,' said Tucker. 'She doesn't need to know.' He turned to Gail. 'Now, darling, bring me the doctor. I've got some questions.'

'Well, Dr Kennedy and Dr Casey are very busy,' said Gail. 'I can ...'

'Did you hear me?' shouted Tucker. 'I want the doctor. Now!'

Gail walked away. Tucker and the other man weren't worried about Alex. They were worried about the concert tour. She went to the lift. The door opened and Dr Kennedy came out.

'How is he?' she asked.

'He's not very good,' he said. 'Where are the two men who are with him?'

'They're over there,' said Gail. 'The short one's his manager. They're not very nice!'

'Right,' said Dr Kennedy. He went towards Mr Tucker.

'Are you the doctor?' said Tucker.

'Yes. Good evening, I'm Dr Ken ...'

'Right. I want a private hospital, not this one,' said Tucker. 'When can we move him?'

'You can't,' said Dr Kennedy. 'His back is broken, and he's in a coma, a deep coma. You can't move him.'

'That's Alex Hayle!' said Tucker angrily. 'He can't stay in a National Health Service hospital with everybody else. We need the best doctors! We need a private hospital.'

'He's got the best doctor,' said Dr Kennedy. 'Dr Casey is a back specialist, and she's …'

'And she's working in a little hospital, in a little town,' said Tucker. 'Look, my friend, Alex Hayle is an international star. He sells millions of CDs and downloads and DVDs every year, and ...'

Dr Kennedy stopped him. 'And he's in a coma, and he's in this hospital. And you're not moving him anywhere. Goodnight.'

He walked quickly back to the lift.

'What's wrong with him?' said Tucker. 'Hey! Nurse! Can you bring us some coffee or something?'

Gail smiled. She was getting some tea for an old lady in the next room. The old lady's husband was in the hospital.

'Mr Tucker,' she said, 'this is a hospital, not a restaurant. There's a coffee machine over there.'

3 Room 534

Gail had to work until six o'clock the next morning. When she got back to the nurses' home, her friends were having breakfast. She told them about the car crash.

'Wow!' said Penny. 'Alex Hayle! I've got downloads of all his songs on a playlist on my computer. It's my favourite playlist, too. Which room is he in?'

'I don't know,' said Gail. 'Look, it's half past six. I'm going to bed! Good night … or is it "Good morning"?'

Gail woke up in the middle of the afternoon. She had to begin work again at ten o'clock on Sunday evening. She turned on the television while she was eating. She wanted to hear the news. There was a video of Alex Hayle on the five o'clock news. Gail turned up the sound.

'That was Alex Hayle, and he was singing *Midnight Party.* Alex is in hospital in Midhurst. He was in a car crash after the concert last night. We spoke to his manager, Clarence Tucker, outside the hospital.'

Gail sat forward in her chair. There was Tucker on the television.

'I saw Alex a few minutes ago. He's going to be all right. He was sitting up in bed, and he was smiling. He can't finish the concert tour, but don't worry! He's going to do another tour next year, so keep your tickets! You can use them next time. I want to thank everyone for the flowers and all the "Get well" cards. Alex is looking at them now. Thank you.'

Gail turned off the television. Alex was going to be all right! But he broke his back. He was in a coma! She couldn't understand. He was sitting up in bed? Was that possible?

At that moment, Penny came in.

'Hey! Gail!' said Penny. 'I saw Alex! He's in Room 534. I work on the fifth floor, you know, and …'

'And is he sitting up and smiling?' asked Gail.

Penny sat down.

'What?' she said.

'Is he sitting up and smiling?'

'He's in a coma,' said Penny. 'He broke his back. You know that.'

'His manager, Mr Tucker, was on television. He said, "Alex is sitting up and smiling".'

'Ah!' said Penny. 'I understand. Dr Casey spoke to us today. We mustn't speak to the newspapers or television about Alex. Tucker spoke to the head of the hospital. You can't see Alex's face, you know. He cut it badly in the crash. And he can't move. It's terrible. It's so sad!'

It wasn't very busy on Sunday evening. At eleven o'clock Gail had to go to the fifth floor for Dr Kennedy. She had to get some medicine. She got the medicine and walked back to the lift. Then she saw the tall man in the black coat. He was standing outside Room 534. She stopped for a moment then walked over to him.

'Hello,' she said.

'Oh, it's you. The nurse from the casualty department.'

'We call it A & E now. Casualty's the old name. What are you doing here?'

'I'm waiting here. Mr Tucker doesn't want any newspaper reporters or TV people near Alex.'

'I know,' said Gail. She thought quickly. 'Excuse me, I'm just going to have a look at him. Dr Kennedy told me to look at him at eleven o'clock. I'm late.'

'The nurse on this floor looked at him ten minutes ago,' said the man.

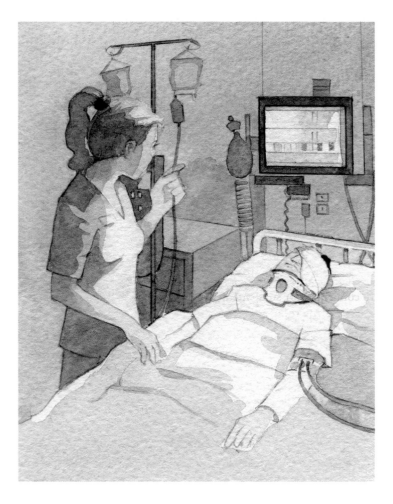

'Yes, I know that,' said Gail. 'Excuse me.'

She opened the door and went in. She closed the door carefully behind her. There was Alex on the bed. He was in a coma. She couldn't see his face. There were a lot of bandages round it. She looked at the machines round the bed. They were fine.

She opened the door and walked out. The head nurse from the fifth floor was there.

'Nurse,' she said, 'can I speak to you? In my office.'

Gail looked at the man in the black coat. He was smiling.

'Er, I have to take this to Dr Kennedy and …'

'I want to speak to you now,' said the head nurse.

They went to the head nurse's office.

'Sit down,' said the head nurse. 'What were you doing in Room 534?'

'Why?' asked Gail. 'Did I do anything wrong?'

'You don't work on this floor. Mr Hayle cannot have any visitors. This afternoon about twenty nurses came to this floor. They all wanted to see him. This is a hospital, not a rock concert.'

'I'm from the A & E department,' said Gail. 'I was there last night … when they brought him in. I was worried about him, and I had to come here for some medicine. Dr Kennedy wanted it … I just looked in the room. I'm sorry.'

'I see,' said the head nurse. 'Well, don't do it again. Do you understand?'

'Yes,' said Gail. 'I'm very sorry.'

She left the office and went towards the lift. The man in the black coat smiled at her.

'Good evening, nurse,' he said, 'and goodbye. I'm not going to see you on this floor again. Right?'

4 A new face

It was two weeks later. Gail was working in the office in the A & E department. The telephone rang. Gail picked it up.

'Accident and emergency,' she said.

'Hello, this is Dr Casey. Could I speak to Dr Kennedy, please?'

'Just a minute,' said Gail. She went and got Dr Kennedy. He came into the office and took the phone. Gail sat down again.

'Kennedy here ... oh, hello, Josephine ... What? ... But they can't! ... They did? ... When? ... No! ... And where are they taking him? ... Why can't they tell you? ... That's terrible! ... Yes, yes ... See you later.'

He put the phone down. He was very angry, Gail could see that. She waited.

'That was Josephine Casey,' he said. 'Mr Tucker took Alex Hayle from the hospital an hour ago.'

'But he's still in a coma!' said Gail.

'Yes. They took him in a private ambulance. They're going to a private hospital. Josephine ... I mean, Dr Casey, is very angry.'

~

Gail often thought about Alex. One evening, a few months later, she was watching television in the nurses' home. It was a rock music programme.

'And now, we've got a new song from Alex Hayle! It's called *Saturday Night,* and here is Alex. He's going to sing it for us. Alex had a car crash a few months ago. He's had plastic surgery ... so it's a new face for *New Face.* As we all remember, Alex was in the group *New Face* two years ago. And so here he is! The wonderful Alex Hayle!'

The music started. There was Alex! Well, his hair was the same, and his clothes were the same, but it was a new face. Plastic surgery? Yes, he cut his face badly, but what about the broken back? What about the coma? Gail listened carefully to the song. Then she stood up.

'That's *not* Alex,' she said. 'It's not!'

Then she thought, 'So where is Alex? What happened to him?'

When Penny came in that evening, Gail spoke to her about Alex. Penny knew all about it.

'It was in the newspaper,' she said. 'They took Alex to Switzerland. He had plastic surgery on his face from a specialist in Geneva.'

'But he broke his back! You know that, Penny. You saw him in hospital.'

'Well, he's fine now,' said Penny. 'I saw him on television yesterday. And he was dancing!'

5 An old friend

The next Saturday, Gail was shopping in Midhurst. She was looking for some new trousers. She went into a clothes shop in the shopping centre and looked at some jeans. Seventy pounds! Everything was very expensive. She stopped and listened to the music in the shop – *Saturday Night*. They were playing the song in all the other clothes shops that afternoon, too. 'It's going to be a big hit, maybe number one,' thought Gail.

'Gail! Hi! How are you?'

Gail turned round. 'Shireen!' she said. 'I'm good. How about you?'

Shireen was an old friend. They were student nurses together in London, five years before.

'Fine. This is great!' said Shireen. 'Come and have a coffee. I want to hear all your news.'

They went to a café and got two coffees. Gail opened her handbag.

'No,' said Shireen, 'let me pay ... really.'

They sat down at a table. Shireen had four or five shopping bags. She put them under the table. 'New clothes,' she said. 'I bought a lovely skirt, a coat and two dresses.'

'What are you doing now?' asked Gail.

'Me? I'm working at a small private hospital. It's near Frampton. It's a wonderful job. The hospital is very expensive, and they pay me very well.'

They talked for half an hour. Shireen was telling Gail about her job.

'I like the job, but it's very sad sometimes,' she said. 'I'm looking after a young man. He had a serious accident a few months ago. He was in a car crash. He broke his back ... and he was in a coma

for several months.'

Gail sat forward. 'He isn't in a coma now?'

'No, he isn't,' said Shireen. 'He woke up two weeks ago. It's very sad. There's something wrong with him. He hurt his head in the crash too. Do you know, he thinks he's that rock star ... the famous one ... he's always on television ... What's his name?'

'Alex Hayle,' said Gail quietly.

'Yes, that's right. He thinks he's Alex Hayle ... but how did you know that?'

'Oh, nothing,' said Gail, 'it was just a guess. Er ... What's the young man's name?'

'Richard Tucker. He can't have any visitors. His brother's a terrible man. He told us ...'

'His brother?'

'Yes. He's a friend of Dr Green. Dr Green is the head of the hospital. Anyway, he doesn't want any visitors. Poor Richard! He cut his face badly in the car crash, you know. He looks terrible, but he's a nice man.'

Gail thought for a moment. 'Er ... Shireen,' she said. 'I'm looking for a new job. Does your hospital need any new nurses?'

'Yes,' said Shireen. 'We always need good nurses. And the private hospital pays a lot more than the National Health Service. Why? Are you ...?'

'I'm not sure. Can I come and see the hospital?'

'OK,' said Shireen. 'Come tomorrow. It's Sunday. Dr Green isn't there on Sundays. You can have a look at the hospital, then maybe you can write to him about a job.'

'Thanks,' said Gail. 'See you tomorrow.'

6 The private hospital

Gail stopped her car and looked at the map. Shireen drew it for her at the café. Yes, this was the road, but where was the hospital? It was somewhere near here. There were tall trees on

both sides of the road, and there were no houses. She looked at the map again. There was no 'H' for 'hospital' sign on the road. She started the car and drove slowly along the road. Then she saw a small road on the left. There was a sign on the corner. It was very small. It said 'Chamford Private Hospital'. Gail turned left and drove along the small road for nearly a mile. Then she saw the hospital. It was a beautiful old house with gardens in front of it.

She drove into the car park and got out of her car. There were several other cars there. They were all expensive – a Rolls-Royce, a Bentley, a Lexus, a Porsche, several Mercedes and BMWs, a Ferrari and some Range Rovers. Gail looked back at her little old Mini and smiled. It looked very funny in the middle of all those big cars.

Shireen was waiting for her near the door. 'You're late,' she said.

'Yes, sorry,' said Gail, 'I couldn't find it. I like your uniform.'

'Mmm,' said Shireen. 'The uniforms are very beautiful. They're very expensive, you know. Maybe it was my map. I can't draw maps very well.'

'I needed the map,' said Gail. 'It's a long way from the village.'

'Yes, it's very quiet here. Very quiet. This is the best time of the day for a visit. We always have visitors on Sunday afternoons.'

'But there are never any visitors for your young man with the cut face,' said Gail. 'What's his name? I don't remember.'

'Richard Tucker,' said Shireen. 'No, he never has visitors. I told you that yesterday. Come on, I'll show you the hospital.'

They walked around the hospital. Everything was new and very expensive. There were flowers everywhere.

'Er ... Where's Richard Tucker?' Gail asked suddenly.

'Why?' said Shireen.

'Oh, I was thinking about him. Can I talk to him for a moment? He doesn't have any visitors. I think that's very sad. He must be very unhappy.'

Shireen smiled. 'All right. Dr Green isn't here. He won't know … Come on, he's upstairs … But just for a minute.'

7 'Richard Tucker'

The room was dark. Gail could see a man on the bed. She went to the light. She was going to turn it on.

'No, don't turn on the light ... please, don't.'

She walked over to the bed. She could see his face. It was terrible.

'All right,' she said. 'Hello, Alex.'

'What did you say?'

'Hello, Alex.'

'But ... the doctors call me Richard. That's not my name. I'm Alex Hayle. You called me Alex ...'

'Yes,' said Gail. She looked at him again. Alex was crying.

'Tell me I'm not crazy ... Am I really Alex Hayle? Tell me seriously ...'

'Yes,' she said. 'You are.' She sat on the bed and took his hand.

'Why am I here? I can't move ... it's my back. I broke my back ... Nobody comes here. Why?'

'Have you got any family?' she asked.

'No. I had an older sister in Australia, but she died five years ago.'

'Tucker said you had no family. So that was true.'

'Tucker? Where's Tucker?' said Alex. 'He can't come in here ... he can't!'

'You're afraid of Tucker?'

Alex was crying again. 'He won't let me leave. Not ever,' he said. 'Who are you? Do you work for Tucker?'

'No, I don't,' said Gail. 'You needn't worry. Don't be afraid. Do you want to get out of here? Really?'

'Yes,' replied Alex quietly. 'More than anything in the world.'

Gail smiled. 'Don't worry,' she said. 'You're going to be out of here ... and in a real hospital tomorrow. I promise.'

She walked to the door. 'I'll see you tomorrow, Alex. Remember, that's a promise. So don't worry.'

Shireen was waiting outside. 'Poor Richard,' she said. 'He's crazy.'

'Yes, poor Richard,' said Gail. 'Excuse me for a moment. I just have to phone someone.'

Gail walked into the beautiful garden. She opened her handbag and took out her phone. She went to the address book, and quickly found the numbers. She put them all in the phone's memory earlier that morning. She pushed the 'Call' key for the first number. That's it! The phone was ringing. A man answered the phone.

'Good afternoon. This is *The Daily News* ...'

'Hello,' said Gail. 'I need to speak to a reporter. I've got an important story for you about Alex Hayle ... and I'm calling every newspaper in the country ...'

Glossary

These extra words are not in the 750 words for Level 2.

A & E department accident and emergency department in a hospital

ambulance a special van that takes people to hospital (see picture)

bandage a long thin piece of white cloth that you put on a cut, or part of your body that hurts (see picture)

bell something that makes a 'ding!' sound when it rings, e.g., a doorbell; the bells in a hospital are electric

casualty someone who is hurt in an accident, or in a war; everyday name for A & E department

coma a very deep sleep, usually for a long time, because of an illness or injury

concert tour a concert is music played in front of a lot of people; a concert tour is when a concert goes from city to city

darling you can say this to someone you love; in the story Tucker is being rude because he is using a friendly word to a stranger

download information (data, programs, music or video) you get from the Internet and move to your computer

emergency when something serious or dangerous happens and people must help

head the most important person in a hospital or school, e.g., head teacher

medicine special drinks or pills that you take when you are ill: *Aspirin is a medicine* (see picture)

midnight twelve o'clock at night

National Health Service in Britain the government pays for hospitals and doctors; everyone can get free medical help

next of kin the closest person in your family, usually your husband or wife or parents, or possibly your children or brothers and sisters

nurse a person whose job is looking after people who are sick or hurt (see picture)

operating theatre a place in a hospital where doctors (surgeons) can work on your body, usually while you are not awake

page one side of a piece of paper in a book or magazine: *There are 40 pages in this book*

paramedic a person who works in an ambulance and is the first one there when there is an accident or emergency (see picture)

patient a person receiving care in a hospital (see picture)

plastic surgery a plastic surgeon can repair or change the look of part of your body, usually your face; they can do this after a bad accident or because somebody wants to look different

playlist a group of songs you put together on a computer: *I have twenty playlists in iTunes*

private not for everybody; the opposite of public; the National Health Service hospitals are public and free, you have to pay at private hospitals

religion believing in God; Christianity, Islam, Buddhism, Hinduism are religions

reporter someone who writes the news stories for newspapers or TV

ring (v) to call someone on the phone; the sound a phone makes before you answer it

serious important and not funny

solo career working alone, not with a group

specialist someone (like a doctor) who knows a lot about one thing, e.g., an eye specialist, an ear specialist, a heart specialist

stadium a place where people play sport and others watch

stretcher a stretcher is used to carry people who are ill and cannot walk (see picture)

visitor someone who visits a place

bell 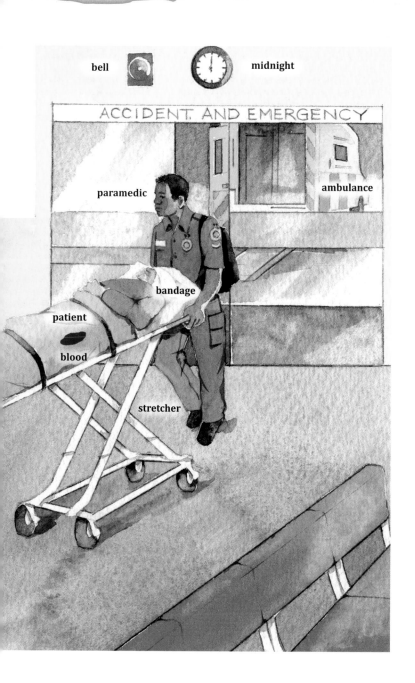 midnight

ACCIDENT AND EMERGENCY

paramedic

ambulance

bandage

patient

blood

stretcher

Activities

1 Look at the story again and find this information. How fast can you find it?

   1   The family name of the back specialist.

   2   The first name of the back specialist.

   3   Alex's real age.

   4   Tucker's address.

   5   Alex's room number at Midhurst Central Hospital.

   6   The city where Gail and Shireen studied nursing.

   7   The name of the private hospital.

   8   The type of car that Gail drives.

2 Are these sentences true (✓) or false (✗)? Correct the false ones.

   1 ☐ Midhurst Hospital is never busy on Saturday evenings.

   2 ☐ Alex left the group *New Face* last September.

   3 ☐ Alex arrived at the hospital on a stretcher.

   4 ☐ Gail got some coffee for Mr Tucker.

   5 ☐ Alex had plastic surgery in Geneva.

   6 ☐ Alex's new record was *Sunday Evening.*

   7 ☐ Gail paid for the coffees when she met her friend, Shireen.

   8 ☐ Shireen gets more money than Gail.

9 ☐ There was a big sign for the private hospital on the road.

10 ☐ Gail telephoned *The Daily News.*

3 Complete the sentences with words from the glossary.

1 Gail works in the _____ department at the hospital.

2 There was a picture of Alex on a _____ in her newspaper.

3 The paramedics carried Alex on a _____.

4 There were _____ round Alex's face.

5 Dr Kennedy went to the _____ theatre.

6 Penny had all of Alex's songs in a _____ on her computer.

7 Midhurst Central Hospital is a public hospital, not a _____ hospital.

8 The _____ nurse was angry because Gail went into Alex's room.

9 Gail went to the fifth floor because Dr Kennedy wanted some _____.

10 Alex had a broken back and was in a _____.

4 Do these comprehension tasks.

1 Why was Saturday night busy at the hospital?

2 Where was Gail reading the newspaper?

3 What kind of accident did Alex have?

4   What happened to him?

5   What questions did Gail ask Mr Tucker?

6   Why couldn't the nurses speak to the newspapers about Alex?

7   Why was the man in the black coat standing outside Alex's room?

8   Who told the head nurse that Gail went into the room?

9   Why were the doctors angry when Tucker took Alex from the hospital?

10 Did Alex really go to Switzerland?

11 Who was singing *Saturday Night* on television?

12 Why did Gail go shopping in Midhurst?

13 Who did she meet?

14 What did Shireen tell Gail about her job?

15 Where was the private hospital?

16 Why was Sunday the best time for a visit?

17 Was the man's name really Richard Tucker?

18 Who was he?

19 When did Gail put the numbers in her phone's memory?

20 Why did she telephone the newspaper?

5 Discuss these questions.

    1 Describe Clarence Tucker. What kind of man was he?

    2 Describe the private hospital.

    3 Why was Alex in the private hospital?

    4 What is going to happen after Gail's phone call? Tell the story.

6 Imagine ...

Who was the man on television (the man singing *Saturday Night*)? Think of a name for him. How did he get the job? How old is he? Is he getting a lot of money? Does he know about the real Alex? Is he really singing?

7 Find the words below in the word square.

bandage	hospital
blood	ill
casualty	nurse
coma	paramedic
doctor	pills
face	stretcher
head	surgery

H	B	B	L	O	O	D	C	O	M	A
C	A	S	U	A	L	T	Y	W	J	O
Y	H	B	A	N	D	A	G	E	J	I
C	E	S	T	R	E	T	C	H	E	R
P	A	R	A	M	E	D	I	C	X	B
C	D	L	I	C	S	N	U	R	S	E
M	N	H	O	S	P	I	T	A	L	P
D	L	D	O	C	T	O	R	V	U	I
C	K	S	U	R	G	E	R	Y	I	L
T	D	F	A	C	E	A	L	F	L	L
G	C	I	X	F	P	O	H	M	L	S

8 Here are the top ten singles for the week *Saturday Night* was on TV. Circle all the words that are the same, or nearly the same in your language.

★**1** | **Alex Hayle** | Play now ▶
| Saturday Night | Buy £

▼**2** | **Heavy Metal Boys** | Play now ▶
| Frankenstein's Monster | Buy £

★**3** | **Girls On TV** | Play now ▶
| World Cup Winners | Buy £

▼**4** | **The Old Guys** | Play now ▶
| Rock 'n' Roll Party | Buy £

▲**5** | **Angela** | Play now ▶
| Why don't you text me? | Buy £

★**6** | **Carlie Logan** | Play now ▶
| Princess of Pop | Buy £

▼**7** | **Drum 'n' Bass Crew** | Play now ▶
| Mozart 2014 | Buy £

▼**8** | **Binary System** | Play now ▶
| 4 Me, 4U | Buy £

▲**9** | **Chilton Hendry** | Play now ▶
| I've Got the Blues, Baby | Buy £

★**10** | **Russell Keeping** | Play now ▶
| Waiting for the Telephone | Buy £

Other titles available in the series

Garnet Oracle — Level 1

The Collector

The Locked Room

The Watchers

Zoo Diary

Garnet Oracle — Level 2

Casualty!

Strawberry and The Sensations

Underground

The Visit

Garnet Oracle — Level 3

African Adventure

Life Lines

Milo

Sunnyvista City

Garnet Oracle — Level 4

The Case of the Dead Batsman

The Hitchhiker

Space Romance

A Tidy Ghost